# HUNT ⬥ KILLER®
## MYSTERY

# THE
# DETECTIVE'S
# PUZZLE BOOK

## TRUE-CRIME-INSPIRED CIPHERS, CODES, AND BRAIN GAMES

ULYSSES PRESS

Published by:
ULYSSES PRESS
PO Box 3440
Berkeley, CA 94703
www.ulyssespress.com

ISBN: 978-1-64604-399-6
Library of Congress Control Number: 2022933299

Printed in the United States by Kingery Printing Company
10 9 8 7 6 5 4 3 2 1

Acquisitions editor: Casie Vogel
Managing editor: Claire Chun
Editor: Kate St.Clair
Proofreader: Renee Rutledge
Interior design and layout: what!design @ whatweb.com
Production: Yesenia Garcia-Lopez
Artwork: from shutterstock.com except Gayle Towell pages 33, 57, 69; Fiverr pages 39, 64, 65, 85

For sleuths, code-crackers,
and puzzle-solvers everywhere

# CONTENTS

**GRAY INVESTIGATIONS**

Hello,

Welcome to *Hunt A Killer: The Detective's Puzzle Book*. First, I want to thank you for your help with my most important cases at Gray Investigations, LLC. But everyone can use some practice, right? I've designed this training manual as a tool to hone your investigative skills between cases. In the following pages, you'll face a variety of challenges, from simple solves to more advanced brainteasers.

These puzzles were designed using details from my previous cases. Each puzzle will offer a scenario and all the necessary hints to solve it.

The challenges in this book are divided into three sections of increasing difficulty. I'll start you off at Aspiring Sleuth (beginner puzzles, page 23) before promoting you to Private Investigator (intermediate puzzles, page 55) and then finally to Lead Detective (advanced puzzles, page 83).

By the end of the book, you will find your mental faculties put to the ultimate test. I've provided some investigative best practices (page 11) that include some tips for successful sleuthing as well as an overview of different ciphers I've seen when people are trying to communicate secrets.

Refer to this whenever you are feeling stuck. All solutions can be found in the back of the book in the order in which they appear. However, to stretch your mind, I advise that you only review the solutions once you're absolutely certain you've already deduced the correct answer.

I'm in need of first-rate sleuths on my team. The kind of investigator who can rise to the challenge, doesn't back down when things get hard, and possesses a curious and sharp mind. The kind of investigator who can solve all of these puzzles.

I believe that's you. Good luck!

*Michelle Gray*

Michelle Gray

# INVESTIGATIVE BEST PRACTICES

Here are some tips, tricks, and strategies to keep in mind as you conduct your investigation:

**1.** Remember to consistently use all of the tools at your disposal.

**2.** Examine every clue, sentence, or piece of evidence very carefully. You never know when an innocuous-seeming phrase will be the key to cracking a code.

**3.** Always keep an eye on the big picture, even when you're combing through the small details. If something isn't lining up right, try to cross-reference it with other facts.

**4.** Always take notes on your findings. Feel free to underline, write on, or highlight the text. Any piece of information, no matter how inconsequential it may seem at first, could prove crucial in cracking the case wide open.

## CODES AND CIPHERS GUIDE

Throughout this training guide, you might come across a few codes and ciphers. People with things to hide tend not to leave their secrets sitting out in the open unprotected. I've created this list to help crack some of the most common cipher types.

## ABJAD

This is less a form of cipher and more a system of writing, but I've seen it used to encode information plenty of times in the past. In simple terms, it's the omission of vowels from the text. Sometimes the writer will replace the vowels with a neutral symbol.

If you come across a word written in abjad that could be read several different ways depending on the missing vowels, try looking at the big picture. Context clues can be a lifesaver when you're trying to decipher messages written in this format.

Written in abjad, the word example would look like this:

- xmpl

- -x-mpl-

## ATBASH CIPHER

In an atbash cipher, the alphabet is mapped onto itself backward.

Here's a chart that shows what I mean:

| A | B | C | D | E | F | G | H | I | J | K | L | M |
|---|---|---|---|---|---|---|---|---|---|---|---|---|
| Z | Y | X | W | V | U | T | S | R | Q | P | O | N |

| N | O | P | Q | R | S | T | U | V | W | X | Y | Z |
|---|---|---|---|---|---|---|---|---|---|---|---|---|
| M | L | K | J | I | H | G | F | E | D | C | B | A |

In an atbash cipher, the word *example* would be: vcznkov.

## BOOK CIPHER

A book cipher needs to be used in conjunction with a pretty large section of text. This text might be found on a separate piece of paper from the code itself *or* on the same page.

The cipher tells the reader what words or letters *within* a passage to look at, and in what order, to find a hidden message.

The text can be anything from a letter to the page of a book to a shopping list, so be vigilant!

To decode a book cipher, be on the lookout for anything that might indicate on what line of a page, what word in a line, or what letter in a word you should focus.

If I wanted to call your attention to the word *example* in the following text, I could do it by providing you with the location of the word itself with this key: (2/7).

He was exacting in his standards and minimal in his praise.

He always strove to lead by example.

The key (2/7) indicates the location of the hidden word. The word *example* is on the second line. It is the seventh word of that line.

I could scatter the information even further by providing you with something like this, which gives you the necessary information in the format of **line/word/letter**:

1/1/2 1/3/2 1/6/3 1/8/1 1/11/1 2/5/1 2/7/7

H**e** was e**x**acting in his st**a**ndards and **m**inimal in his **p**raise.

He always strove to **l**ead by exampl**e**.

When read in order, the letters indicated by the key spell out the word *example*.

## CAESAR SHIFT CIPHER

This cipher name is based on the belief that Julius Caesar used it to encrypt his personal communications. To encode a sentence using a shift cipher, the writer shifts each letter of the alphabet forward by a certain fixed number.

For example, the top row of the following chart is the regular, unencoded alphabet. The bottom row is the alphabet shifted forward by five letters.

| A | B | C | D | E | F | G | H | I | J | K | L | M |
|---|---|---|---|---|---|---|---|---|---|---|---|---|
| F | G | H | I | J | K | L | M | N | O | P | Q | R |

| N | O | P | Q | R | S | T | U | V | W | X | Y | Z |
|---|---|---|---|---|---|---|---|---|---|---|---|---|
| S | T | U | V | W | X | Y | Z | A | B | C | D | E |

The word *example* shifted forward by five letters is jcfruqj.

To decode jcfruqj, you must shift each individual letter backward by five places in the alphabet.

The alphabet can be shifted by any number, although shifting by numbers greater than 26 can get a bit redundant (since, of course, the English alphabet only has 26 letters). In other words, shifting by 27 would be the same as shifting by one, shifting by 28 would be the same as shifting by two, and so on.

Remember: there are plenty of ways to add complexity to a shift cipher. Because of this, not all shift ciphers will appear to be straightforward. Here are a few examples of potential complications you might encounter when decoding shift ciphers:

- The shift is only used on parts of the message. Perhaps every second word is shifted, while the other words in a sentence are left alone. This can also be done by letter. For example, every third letter might be shifted, while the rest of the message is left alone.

- More than one shift is used within the same message. For example, one sentence in a message could be shifted by 12, while the next sentence is shifted by seven. On a more difficult level, this could even occur within the words themselves. Perhaps every even letter is shifted by two, while every odd letter is shifted by four.

- The shifted word itself is spelled backward or scrambled in some other manner.

- On the most difficult level, you might encounter a cipher that is layered over another cipher. In this case, you might decode a phrase into a nonsensical answer and then have to decipher it again by some additional method that is discovered in a separate place from the original key.

- To find the key to a shift cipher, look around for numbers that seem like they've been highlighted in some way or numbers that might be relevant to the cipher's writer. For example, you might find an underlined digit or a birthday. The number might be explicitly written out, or it might be hidden as part of an image or symbol. The clue might be in a painting that has 5 birds or 12 trees, telling you the shift number is 5 or 12, respectively. If you can't find a key, you can always try to "brute force" a cipher by running it through an online decryption service.

- A common variant of a Caesar shift is the date cipher. A date cipher uses a repeating number (usually a date) as the key to the shift. To encode a message with a date cipher, the numbers of the date are written above the message, with each letter being assigned one number from the date. If the message is longer than the date number, the date number is repeated as many times as necessary to reach the end of the message. For example, let's say our message to encode is "This is a date cipher." And the date to be used is December 25, 2001. The shift number is then 12252001. So we would shift *T* by 1, *h* by 2, *i* by 2, *s* by 5, and so on. When we reach the end of the date (shifting *d* by 1), we simply start the number over again and repeat the process (shifting *a* by 1, *t* by 2, etc.) Our final encoded message is then: Ujkx ks a ebvg hkphfs. A full date is not needed to use a date cipher. It can be only a day and month, or just a year, or even a string of numbers that isn't actually a date at all but uses the same encoding process.

# KEYPAD CIPHER

The basic idea of this cipher is to assign all of the letters of the alphabet to specific places on a grid like this one:

| ABC | DEF | GHI |
|-----|-----|-----|
| JKL | MNO | PQR |
| STU | VWX | YZ  |

You might notice that it looks like the keypad of a telephone. While this example organizes the alphabet onto a 3x3 grid reminiscent of a phone, the alphabet can be spread across grids of any organization: 5x2, 3x6, and so on.

Once the writer has assigned letters to places on the grid, there must be some kind of shorthand to refer to the physical position of each letter on the grid.

Keep in mind that these grids don't necessarily have to start with *A* in the upper right-hand corner. You may need to determine how the alphabet is supposed to fall on the grid before you can start decoding.

To decode a keypad cipher, look for notes that might indicate the position of a specific letter. For example, since *A* is the first letter in the box that would be mapped onto the number *1* on a typical keypad (the model for my grid above), one way to denote its position would be 1-1. By the same logic, *E* would be 2-2, since it is the second letter in the second box.

The word *example* spelled out this way is therefore: 2-2 8-3 1-1 5-1 6-1 4-3 2-2.

## SYMBOL SUBSTITUTION CIPHER

A symbol substitution cipher uses symbols to represent different letters. The most common version of this cipher uses a one-to-one relationship, where one letter is represented by one symbol. To solve this type of cipher, look for short sections of symbols, usually 1 to 3 symbols long. Then try plugging in common words to see if you can determine if there are any likely symbol-letter pairs. This method requires a good bit of trial and error, but the code should reveal itself eventually. Sometimes there are keys or patterns to how the symbols are assigned, and if you are able to figure out that pattern, you will not have to use trial and error as much. If there seems to be a unifying theme or order to the symbols, that is a good sign that there is a key that can be used to make cracking the code more straightforward than simply guessing and checking.

For more information on all the previous ciphers discussed, check out these websites:

- http://practicalcryptography.com/ciphers/caesar-cipher

- https://cryptii.com

# ADDITIONAL PUZZLES GUIDE

In this book you will also come across several puzzles that are not cipher-related. The below is a list of the additional puzzle types and some accompanying information to help you solve them.

## CRITICAL READING LOGIC PUZZLES

These puzzles require special attention to detail. Written as a conversation between investigators exchanging crime scene details, it's your job to determine which facts align with which victims.

## LOGIC GRID PUZZLES

Logic puzzles have several categories with an equal number of possible options for each. In order to solve the ones in this book, I've provided a grid to cross-reference the possible options in each category. Each option is used only one time. You need to determine which categories and options are linked together based on the given clues. You can eliminate pairs you know aren't possible with an *X*, and mark pairs you know are linked with an *O*. After doing this for each of the given clues, you will be able to deduce the solution to the puzzle. These puzzles are solved using simple logic, and there is only one correct solution for each puzzle.

Example:

| | MOTIVE | | | | TIME | | | | HOUSE COLOR | | | |
|---|---|---|---|---|---|---|---|---|---|---|---|---|
| | Annabelle | Heather | Kassidy | Tatum | 8:00 a.m. | 12:00 p.m. | 5:00 p.m. | 12:00 a.m. | Blue | Cyan | Lime | Purple |
| **SALARY** $55,000 | | X | | X | X | | | | X | O | X | X |
| $128,000 | | | | | | | | | X | X | | |
| $144,000 | | X | X | | | | | | | X | | |
| $158,000 | | | X | | | | | | | X | | . |
| **HOUSE COLOR** Blue | X | | X | | | X | | | | | | |
| Cyan | O | X | X | X | | X | | | | | | |
| Lime | X | X | | X | X | O | X | X | | | | |
| Purple | X | | | X | | X | | | | | | |
| **PRESCRIPTION** Benazepril | | | | | | | | | | | | |
| Enalapril | | X | | X | | | | | | | | |
| Fosinopril | | | | | | | | | | | | |
| Ramipril | X | | | | | | | | | | | |

## MAZE PUZZLES

Follow paths through different scenarios to find an exit. Think carefully, as some mazes might have a singular rule or pattern that determines how to solve them.

## SPOT-THE-DIFFERENCE PUZZLES

These puzzles call for a careful eye, a crucial skill for determining if a crime scene or evidence has been tampered with. The two pictures may appear identical at first, but things aren't always as they appear. Study the first picture carefully, then determine what 10 key changes were made in the second picture. The differences could be things that are missing, added, and sometimes even just moved the tiniest bit.

## SUSPECT/WITNESS PUZZLES

Review the summary of the crime and study the statements made by three key witnesses or suspects. Read their testimony carefully and take notes if needed, as there may be incorrect facts or details provided that don't add up. Feel free to do some internet research if you feel stuck.

For example, say a suspect or witness claims that their alibi involved caring for their saltwater aquarium that is filled with clown fish, butterfly fish, and neon tetra fish. Some quick research will show that neon tetra fish are freshwater fish and do not go in saltwater tanks. This would expose this alibi as a lie.

# WORD LADDER PUZZLES

These puzzles challenge you to morph the first word into the last word by changing only one letter at a time. Write each new word with the changed letter on each step of the ladder. Each new word must be a common English word, and the order of the letters cannot be changed. There are many ways to solve a word ladder. The provided solutions offer one way, but don't be surprised if you can figure out other words that bring you to the bottom of the ladder. Can you get to the last word before you run out of steps?

Example:

HEAD

HEAL

TEAL

TELL

TALL

TAIL

# ASPIRING SLEUTH: BEGINNER PUZZLES

# THE FLIP PHONE CONUNDRUM

A key piece of evidence in an ongoing murder investigation seems to have stumped investigators. A note was found on the victim's nightstand, lying underneath an old cell phone. But the note is in some sort of code that no one has been able to crack. Using the information below, can you solve this mysterious code?

9-1, 4-3, 7-3, 3-2

8-1, 4-2, 3-2

6-1, 6-3, 6-2, 3-2, 9-3

3-3, 4-3, 7-3, 7-4, 8-1

6-3, 3-3

3-1, 3-2, 2-3, 3-2, 6-1, 2-2, 3-2, 7-3.

8-2, 7-4, 3-2

8-1, 4-2, 4-3, 7-4

7-1, 4-2, 6-3, 6-2, 3-2

8-1, 6-3

2-3, 6-3, 6-2, 8-1, 2-1, 2-3, 8-1

9-2, 2-1, 8-3, 4-3, 3-2, 7-3.

# TRIPLE HOMICIDE AT THE SUNSET MOTEL

On the scene of a triple homicide at The Sunset Motel in Garfield, Nevada, Detective Metzger identifies the victims as Skyler Green, Alex Brown, and Tracy Gray.

Detective Aldin notes, "Isn't it funny how one victim is wearing a green shirt, another is wearing a brown shirt, and another is wearing a gray shirt—just like their names?"

"I suppose," says Detective Metzger, "But none of their shirt colors match their names."

"Is Skyler the woman?" asks Detective Aldin, pointing to the one female victim, who is not wearing a green shirt.

"No," says Detective Metzger. "Skyler is one of two male victims."

"Is the one with the gray shirt Alex Brown?" asks Detective Aldin.

"No," says Detective Metzger.

Which of the victims is female, and what shirt color is each wearing?

# "CRIME TIME"

Five criminals (Clyde Danger, Micky Mongoose, Florida Rose, Teddy Oswald, and Patty Manson) have each been sentenced to prison for an assault crime outside the Cadence Theater. However, each criminal was sentenced by a different judge (Judge Brown, Judge Garcia, Judge Anderson, Judge Lee, or Judge Campbell), and each received a different sentence length (1, 3, 5, 7, or 10 years). Use the following clues to determine which judge passed which sentence for each criminal.

**1.** Judge Brown gave the most lenient sentence and Judge Anderson never sentences anyone to more than 5 years for assault.

**2.** If you add the length of Clyde Danger's sentence to the length of Teddy Oswald's sentence, you get the length of Patty Manson's sentence.

**3.** Judge Garcia, who passed a 5-year prison sentence, was not Florida Rose's judge.

**4.** The criminals include Clyde Danger; the criminal sentenced by Judge Lee; and the criminal who was given 3 years in prison.

|  |  | JUDGE | | | | | SENTENCE | | | | |
|---|---|---|---|---|---|---|---|---|---|---|---|
|  |  | Judge Brown | Judge Garcia | Judge Anderson | Judge Lee | Judge Campbell | 1 year | 3 years | 5 years | 7 years | 10 years |
| **CRIMINAL** | Clyde Danger | | | | | | | | | | |
| | Micky Mongoose | | | | | | | | | | |
| | Florida Rose | | | | | | | | | | |
| | Teddy Oswald | | | | | | | | | | |
| | Patty Manson | | | | | | | | | | |
| **SENTENCE** | 1 year | | | | | | | | | | |
| | 3 years | | | | | | | | | | |
| | 5 years | | | | | | | | | | |
| | 7 years | | | | | | | | | | |
| | 10 years | | | | | | | | | | |

# GUNNING FOR ANSWERS

You're going undercover to try to infiltrate an illegal firearms ring, and you're posing as an arms dealer that police captured earlier. But right before you leave for a top secret meeting that police hope will lead you to the mastermind behind the ring, you learn that there's a password to get into the meeting. The arms dealer isn't talking, so you and the police go back through all your evidence to try to find a clue. Your search leads you to an encrypted file named "Reverse" on the arms dealer's laptop, which turns out to be a strange document filled with what looks like gibberish. You're positive this is the password—you just need to decode it before it's too late!

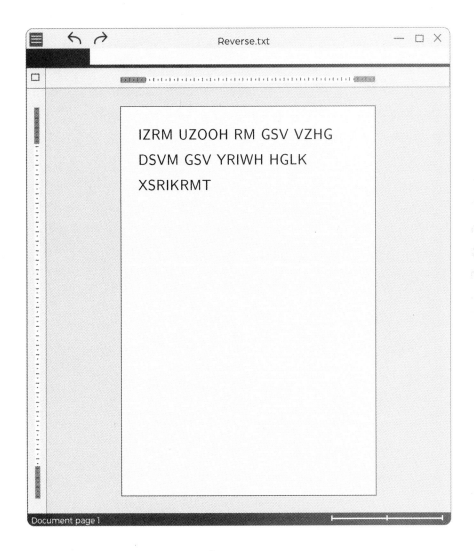

Reverse.txt

IZRM UZOOH RM GSV VZHG
DSVM GSV YRIWH HGLK
XSRIKRMT

Document page 1

# AN A-MAZING FINGERPRINT

The fingerprint on the next page was found at a crime scene. A lab technician blew it up and noticed that it made a nice maze. Starting at the star in the middle, can you find your way out of the fingerprint?

# SHOT TO DEATH

Detective Alva is questioning three suspects in the death of a local physician named Dr. Fontaine, who was shot to death in his driveway after coming home late from work. The suspects are the doctor's wife, Mrs. Fontaine, a colleague of the doctor, Dr. Bass, and a patient, Mr. Norton.

Dr. Fontaine left work at 9:08 p.m. according to video footage outside his office. The drive from his office to home takes about 15 minutes. 9-1-1 received several calls from neighbors at around 9:25 p.m., but no one saw anything.

Mrs. Fontaine was home alone when her husband pulled into the driveway. She says she heard the shot as well, but went outside first instead of calling. This is when she found her husband lying in the driveway, bleeding.

It is widely known that Dr. Bass and Dr. Fontaine had a serious rivalry. In fact, Dr. Fontaine recently received an award that Dr. Bass felt he himself deserved instead, and he said as much to a whole crowd at the award ceremony. "No, I didn't like Dr. Fontaine," says Dr. Bass when questioned. "But I would never kill him. I was home alone all that evening, from 7:00 p.m. until morning."

Mr. Norton recently left Dr. Fontaine's office upset because the doctor refused to prescribe painkillers and instead referred him to drug rehab. "But I've turned a corner since then," says Mr. Norton. "I was out for an evening jog from 9:00 p.m. until 10:00 p.m. that night."

Mrs. Fontaine demands that the detective arrest Mr. Norton. "It had to be him," she says. "He only lives a couple miles away and could have jogged to our house. He told my husband he would regret not giving him the prescription. He threatened him!"

"But that was a month ago," says Detective Alva. "Why would he wait so long?"

"Maybe he had to plan it first," says Mrs. Fontaine. "He was out, supposedly jogging, at the exact time my husband was shot!"

"I always go jogging at the same time every night now," says Mr. Norton. "And I don't go anywhere near where Dr. Fontaine lives when I do. You really should be looking into Dr. Bass more. Everyone knows he hated Dr. Fontaine."

"I was watching the 9:00 news when the shooting happened," says Dr. Bass. "I can tell you every news story—they were reporting live on a warehouse fire. I promise. I had nothing to do with Dr. Fontaine's murder."

"He could have read all of that same news online later," says Mr. Norton. "What time was that fire, anyway?"

"I know the fire was before 9:15," says Mrs. Fontaine. "I know because I was watching the news myself and that's what time it was when I heard the gunshot."

**Which suspect is lying?**

# A PLAN TO KILL

Change just one letter on each line to go from the top word to the bottom word. Do not change the order of the letters. You must have a common English word at each step.

P L A N

FIAN

FIAT

FEAT

FEIT

FELL

FILL

K I L L

# CRIME AT COPPER CLIFFS

There has been a murder at a home in Copper Cliffs, Arizona. After visiting the house twice in several hours, detectives realized someone had tampered with the crime scene. Luckily there is a photo of the original scene, but they need your help finding what evidence has been removed or added since then. Compare the original photo with the current photo of the crime scene, and look out for 10 key differences.

# THE ART OF THE CRIME

You're assisting police in the murder investigation of a famous art collector. They have arrested the art collector's daughter as the prime suspect, but you don't believe she committed the crime. Later, you find a coded message in the back of the daughter's diary, and you're hoping it could be the key to proving her innocence. Can you decode the cipher from the diary on the next page?

"TF BUJSL PZ MYHTPUN

TL. JOLJR OPZ ZHMLAF

KLWVZPA IVE HA NVSKLU

ILSS IHUR. FVB DPSS

MPUK ZVTL VM AOL

TPZZPUN HYA ZAVSLU

MYVT TF TVAOLY DOLU

ZOL KPLK."

# MURDER GONE A-RYE

Police are reopening the unsolved murder of a local bakery owner after a new piece of evidence came to the light. The evidence was a small note, found in a hidden safe in one of the walls of the old bakery. However, the note seems to be in some sort of code, the only recognizable part being the date written at the top. Could the date be a clue to uncovering a secret message?

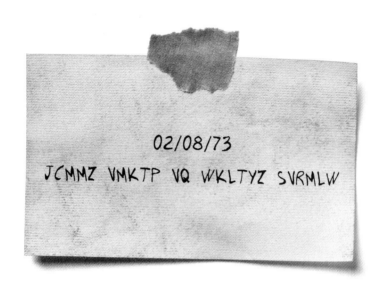

# WRITTEN IN BLOOD

At the scene of a murder, the following coded message was written on the walls in the victim's blood. Officers on the scene found a scrap of paper with a partial key. Using the key, can you decode the message?

Message:

Partial Key:

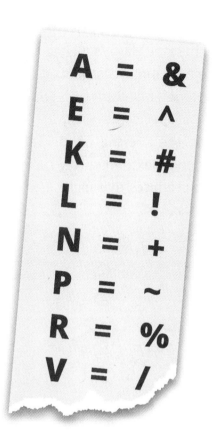

A = &
E = ^
K = #
L = !
N = +
P = ~
R = %
V = /

# SOMEONE IS GUILTY—BAR NONE

There was a robbery at Hardy's Bar, a local favorite in Mallory Rock, Maine. Employees noticed the money had been stolen sometime after closing on Friday night. Police questioned three suspects the following day: Amy, the bartender working the evening of the robbery; Stan, a patron at the bar; and Alexa, an unruly customer who was asked to leave the premises that night. They collected the following statements:

**Amy:** Last night was rough. I worked until closing, and I had some particularly difficult customers at the bar. One girl had already had a lot to drink when she came in and sat at the bar. She ordered a couple of Long Island Iced Teas and grew increasingly belligerent until finally we had to kick her out. Not long after that I closed the bar for the night and when I opened it again today, the money was gone.

**Stan:** I had a few beers at Hardy's around midnight. An intoxicated girl came in and sat next to me and kept going on about how rude the bartender was being to her. She kept asking me if I wanted a sip of her drink. It looked like a Long Island Iced Tea. I politely declined and then left. I heard she got kicked out later that night.

**Alexa:** I hate Hardy's Bar. The bartender was completely rude to me last night. I came in and only had like two drinks—nothing with hard liquor in it. Then they asked me to leave! It was completely unfair how they treated me. I'm never going back there again.

After reviewing the witness statements, investigators were able to determine that one of the suspects wasn't being truthful about the events of that night. Which witness was lying, and how did they know?

# THE MOTEL MYSTERY

Charlie Forest, owner of a local motel, is up to something. Lately, suspicious people have been dropping by the motel at all hours of the night, and police believe the motel owner might be connected to a local crime syndicate. As you're staking out the motel one night, you see Charlie open a piece of mail, read it, then light the piece of paper on fire and toss it in a nearby trash can. Once Charlie disappears back inside the motel, you run to the trash can and put out the flames. You're left with only the last few lines of a letter, but it looks like it's written in some sort of code. Try decoding the message and find out if Charlie is really up to something.

TH SHPMNT SHLD B RDY T FR N TH MRNNG N STRDY. LT TH BSS KNW.

# CYBER WARFARE

Amateur cyber attacks have been happening to major businesses across the small town of Brittany Beach, and police are searching for the culprit. The first cyber attacks took place on the following dates: 1/1, 1/10, 5/2, 5/5, 6/9, 7/2, 7/3, 11/1, 11/2, 11/3.

After each attack, the hacker left a strange message on the website of the business he hacked. Each message was only a few seemingly random sentences, and apart they didn't mean much. But when police put all the sentences together, they found a long quote from the novel *Crime and Punishment* by Fyodor Dostoevsky. Does the quote contain some sort of clue? Using all the information you know about these crimes, try decoding the hacker's message to perhaps get one step closer to catching him!

"I want to attempt a thing like that and am frightened by these trifles," he thought, with an odd smile. "Hm... yes, all is in a man's hands and he lets it all slip from cowardice, that's an axiom. It would be interesting to know what it is men are most afraid of. Taking a new step, uttering a new word is what they fear most.... But I am talking too much. It's because I chatter that I do nothing. Or perhaps it is that I chatter because I do nothing. I've learned to chatter this last month, lying for days together in my den thinking... of Jack the Giant Killer. Why am I going there now? Am I capable of that? Is that serious? It is not serious at all. It's simply a fantasy to amuse myself; a plaything! Yes, maybe it is a plaything."

# SUSPICIOUS SALES

After investigating several local robberies over the past week, police suspect some stolen items may have been sold to Manny's Pawnshop. In an effort to identify the robbers, police interviewed the following witnesses who were involved with the shop, and who saw a male suspect sell a large number of items. The witnesses include: Danielle, an employee of the pawnshop; Alex, a customer; and Johnny, Danielle's 11-year-old son who is often on the pawnshop premises after school. Police collected the following witness statements:

**Danielle:** Yes, I saw a guy come in with a lot of electronics and jewelry. He was tall, with dark hair and a mustache. I processed all the sales, and he left quickly—hardly said a word to me. From the window I saw him get into a minivan and drive away. I didn't think much of it. I processed a lot of sales that day, but I would know the guy if I saw him again.

**Alex:** I was waiting in line behind another guy to sell at the pawn shop. His sale took a while, he had a lot of items. Laptops, tablets, jewelry, all kinds of things. He finally left with what I imagine is a good amount of money, and that was the last I saw of him. Didn't get a very good look, but he was a tall guy. Drove away in something that was incredibly noisy in the parking lot.

**Johnny:** My mom was busy at the register with some tall guy who had a lot of stuff to sell, so I took my bicycle out to the parking lot and rode around. Sometimes when I'm bored I count how many cars are in the parking lot. It was a busy day, so there were lots. I counted 4 cars, 3 trucks, and 1 motorcycle. The motorcycle was really cool, but I went back inside before I could see who owned it. I heard it leave though, it was super loud!

After reviewing these statements, police determined that one of the witnesses was not being truthful and subjected them to further questioning. Which witness was lying and how did they know?

# PRIVATE INVESTIGATOR: INTERMEDIATE PUZZLES

# ESCAPE THE MAZE

A serial killer likes to trap his victims in a maze made of tall thorn bushes. The victims are placed in the center, and if they are unable to escape fast enough, the killer activates a series of trapdoors that drop his victims into a dungeon below. Can you find your way out of the maze?

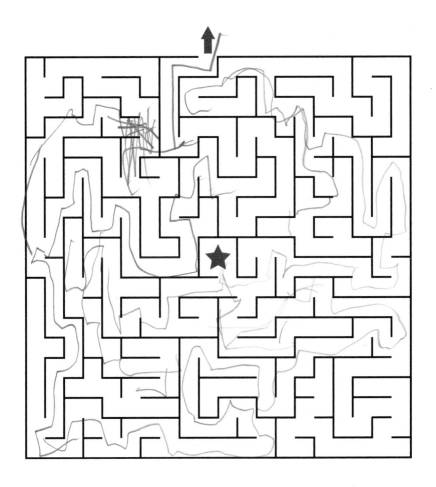

# ART OF THE STEAL

The police are investigating an art theft at the home of private art collector George Hartly. Several paintings and a jade vase have gone missing, but the only evidence that someone broke in is a broken glass door at the back of the house. Police suspect Hartly may have had something to do with his own robbery to collect the insurance on the art, but they don't have enough evidence to prove it. As you begin investigating Hartly, you come across a book of poetry by T. S. Eliot. One page has a strange number sequence below the poem titled "Aunt Helen." What could it mean?

# Aunt Helen

Miss Helen Slingsby was my maiden aunt,

And lived in a small house near a fashionable square

Cared for by servants to the number of four.

Now when she died there was silence in heaven

And silence at her end of the street.

The shutters were drawn and the undertaker wiped his feet—

He was aware that this sort of thing had occurred before.

The dogs were handsomely provided for,

But shortly afterwards the parrot died too.

The Dresden clock continued ticking on the mantelpiece,

And the footman sat upon the dining-table

Holding the second housemaid on his knees—

Who had always been so careful while her mistress lived.

1.3.5, 2.7.4, 2.9.6, 3.4.4, 3.7.5, 4.3.1, 4.5.1, 5.6.1,
6.7.10, 7.3.1, 7.8.5, 8.5.7, 9.1.2, 10.2.7, 10.5.2,
11.2.1, 11.5.4, 12.4.8, 13.4.4, 13.10.4

# A MURDERER, WITH BLOOD ON THEIR HANDS, FRETS

Change just one letter on each line to go from the top word to the bottom word. Do not change the order of the letters. You must have a common English word at each step.

BLOOD

BRood

BRoad

Bread

Tread

Tree~~d~~

Trees

Frees

FRETS

# TERROR POSTSCRIPT

Someone has been scaring the residents of Banbury, England, by leaving threatening letters in their mailboxes. Each letter is accompanied by a coded message that no one has been able to crack. Despite each letter being left in mailboxes on different days, they were all written on the same date: September 25, '16. Try decoding the message to get one step closer to stopping this mysterious letter writer.

QHTXCKT KIOUKGSTQ XONQ BN COI
GUC CKHTRN UNGS
CJUIJ RE RG EQZ CJO.

# THE BAFFLING BANK CODE

A bank heist just took place at United American Financial Bank, and the perpetrators successfully got away with more than $1 million. Despite police devoting all available resources to this case for the past week, there are still no leads. You come in to assist on the case, and after a few days of digging through the backgrounds of every United American Financial Bank employee, you finally discover what may be a huge lead—a bizarre deleted email on the bank manager's private email account. But it's written in a weird code. Could this be a clue?

To: anonymous

Cc:

From: United American Financial Bank                               Bcc

Jn lvnth sms fn dy fr sm fn n th r. Th scrty
systm s bng rprd t nn nd th cmrs wll b
dwn. Bt nly fr tn mnts, thn bck t nrml.
lck n th bck dr hs ls bn gvng mntnnc sm
prblms ltly.

Send                                                    🗑 | ▼

# OFFICE EVIDENCE

A detective's office has been tampered with, and they need your help finding what evidence has been removed or added since then. Compare the original photo with the current photo of the office, and look out for 10 key differences.

# LATE NIGHT AT THE LIBRARY

At Atlantic Coast State University, a student named Kathy goes missing. She was last seen walking alone out of the school library on the night of November 1st. Investigators have decided to question three witnesses who were the last to see Kathy before her disappearance: Roxanne, a university librarian; Alana, a fellow classmate; and David, Kathy's boyfriend. They collected the below statements:

**Roxanne:** I saw Kathy studying with a classmate on the fourth floor. They were working on a paper for a literature course, and she asked me where she could find 18th and 19th century fiction. I directed her, and she and the other student gathered some books and returned to studying. Her companion left around 9 p.m., and Kathy stayed about another half hour before leaving.

**Alana:** Kathy and I worked on a paper for our Romantic Era literature course that night. We were writing about Jane Austen, so we grabbed copies of three of her books: *Pride and Prejudice*, *Sense and Sensibility*, and *The Tenant of Wildfell Hall*. After reviewing these, we finished up the paper, and I left around 9 p.m. Kathy told me she was going to work on some other homework for a bit, and she seemed upset about something. I haven't seen her since.

**David:** I texted Kathy around 9:15 p.m. that night, and she told me she was finishing up some homework.

I told her to come to my apartment afterward, and she said she would. Around 9:30 p.m. I got a text from her saying she was walking over, but she never showed up. I finally called around 10:30 p.m. and she didn't answer. That's the last contact I had with her.

After reviewing the witness statements, investigators were able to determine that one of the suspects was lying about the events of that night, and subjected them to further questioning. Which witness was lying, and how did they know?

# FIND THE BODY

A serial killer sent the following puzzle to the local newspaper, asking it to be printed. The killer states in his letter to the paper:

> I've done it again! I've killed another one. Want to find the body? Solve the puzzle! Starting at the letter G, you must trace a path through all of the letters, being sure to pass through each letter of the location only once. If you pass through the letters in the right order, it spells out the location where I've stashed the body. Can you find it?

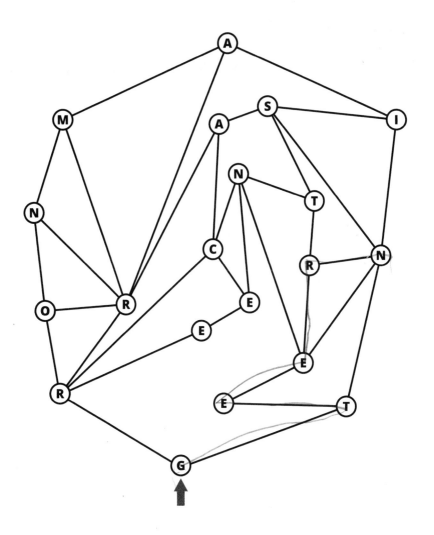

Bowman Grove Amusement Park is gearing up for its yearly Halloween festival, but someone keeps vandalizing the amusement park rides. The vandal leaves cryptic messages at each vandalism site, but no one has been able to figure out what they mean. Clearly someone doesn't want this Halloween festival to happen, but why? Could the below cryptic message be a clue?

DSB, LS DSB, NFHG BLF XVOVYIZGV

SZOOLDVVM? GSV DLIHG SLORWZB LU

GSV BVZI RH NVZMG GL YV LYHVIEVW RM

HROVMXV ZMW DRGSLFG UZMUZIV. GSV

UVHGREZO NFHG HGLK. LI VOHV.

Jake Morgan from the boy band Just4Fun has been kidnapped. His manager, Rachel Day, received the following encrypted ransom note. Rachel thinks the longest encrypted word in the letter is most likely "Pennsylvania." Can you decrypt the message and find out what the kidnappers want?

EWSYT COT NGWWGCO ICWWSQU

GO UNSWW DONSQXTI MGWWU OTAZ

ZC ETQQR'U NCODNTOZ GO WSXT

TQGT, ETOOURWPSOGS, MR NGIOGVJZ

ZCOGVJZ, CQ RCDQ MCR KSXT GU

ITSI.

# AFTERNOON ALIBIS

In one afternoon, a series of crimes were committed across Mallory Rock, Maine. The crimes included theft, assault, arson, forgery, and murder, and each was committed at the top of an hour in the afternoon (1:00 p.m., 2:00 p.m., 3:00 p.m., 4:00 p.m., or 5:00 p.m.). Most of the criminals (Frederick, Mary, Eliza, Jonathan, and Mark) had alibis for at least part of the afternoon, though one had no alibi at all. (All of the alibis checked out, so that none of the criminals could have committed a crime during the time covered by their alibi.) Use the following clues to determine which criminal committed which crime at what time, and what their alibi was (attending a party, going on a date, at work, visiting parents, or no alibi) for the other crimes.

**1.** Theft was the last crime committed that day, and the murder occurred before the arson.

**2.** Mary had an alibi until 3:00 p.m., but the person who committed a crime at 3:00 p.m. had no alibi for the entire day.

**3.** The criminal who was on a date for part of the afternoon could not have committed assault or arson, which happened immediately after the assault.

**4.** Either Frederick or Mark is the murderer, though both have alibis covering their time from 3:00 p.m. through 5:00 p.m.

**5.** Jonathan was on a date from 1:00 p.m. until 4:30 p.m.

**6.** The forger was at a party until 3:30 p.m., and the murderer was visiting parents at 2:00 p.m.

**7.** Mark did not commit assault.

| | CRIME | | | | |
|---|---|---|---|---|---|
| | Theft | Assault | Arson | Forgery | Murder |
| **CRIMINAL** Frederick | | | | | |
| Mary | | | | | |
| Eliza | | | | | |
| Jonathan | | | | | |
| Mark | | | | | |
| **TIME OF CRIME** 1:00 p.m. | | | | | |
| 2:00 p.m. | | | | | |
| 3:00 p.m. | | | | | |
| 4:00 p.m. | | | | | |
| 5:00 p.m. | | | | | |
| **ALIBI** Party | | | | | |
| Date | | | | | |
| Work | | | | | |
| Parents | | | | | |
| None | | | | | |

|  | ALIBI | | | | | TIME OF CRIME | | | |
| --- | --- | --- | --- | --- | --- | --- | --- | --- | --- |
| | Party | Date | Work | Parents | None | 1:00 p.m. | 2:00 p.m. | 3:00 p.m. | 4:00 p.m. | 5:00 p.m. |
| | | | | | | | | | | |
| | | | | | | | | | | |
| | | | | | | | | | | |
| | | | | | | | | | | |
| | | | | | | | | | | |
| | | | | | | | | | | |
| | | | | | | | | | | |
| | | | | | | | | | | |
| | | | | | | | | | | |
| | | | | | | | | | | |

# CURVEBALL CRIME

Starting pitcher for the Thunderbay Tigers baseball team, Gerry Ricks, recently died under mysterious circumstances, but police have ruled it an accidental death. But Gerry's family believes he was murdered, and they suspect it has something to do with the second-string pitcher Ivan Meril. Everyone knows Meril has been upset since he lost the starting pitcher position to Gerry. After digging through some old files in the office of the Thunderbay Tigers' general manager, Hank, you come across a typed letter addressed to Ivan's father. You also find a handwritten note that looks like some sort of coded message. Could this be a clue?

Dear Mr. Meril,

Here's the information you requested on the first-string roster.

| PITCHER<br>- GERRY RICKS | CATCHER<br>- KYLE FITZWILLIAM | FIRST BASE<br>- STEFAN FISCHER |
|---|---|---|
| SECOND BASE<br>- JUSTIN PAVIS | THIRD BASE<br>- TYREL COATES | SHORT STOP<br>- JORDAN HATHWAY |
| LEFT FIELD<br>- DAN MARTINEZ | CENTER FIELD<br>- BENJAMIN GOLD | RIGHT FIELD<br>- ALEC TASSO |

While Ivan isn't our starting pitcher currently, he's a great team player who I'm sure will rise above the ranks with more professional experience under his belt! I'm looking forward to seeing how he grows as a player, and I'm sure you are, too. As for how we develop the lineup for our batting order, this year we're trying an experimental approach. Once a first batter is designated, we simply follow the order of positions as listed above, going left to right, top to bottom. Please let me know if you have any other questions regarding Ivan's first seasons with us.

Best,
Hank

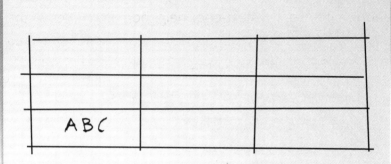

ABC

- C3, C2, CF2
- RF2, SB3, C2, CF1, FB3, CF2, CF1
- SB2, RF2, C3, SB3, SB1, LF1, C2, CF1
- CF3, C3, FB3
- RF2, CF2, P3, FB1
- TB2, RF3, SB2, RF2
- FB3, RF3, LF3, P2, SB1

# GONE IN A NEW YORK MINUTE

A young woman named Alexis went missing in New York City on July 28th. She was last seen leaving the Criterion Arms apartment building, where she lived, at around 7 a.m. Alexis lived alone and was not reported missing until nearly two days later. Police, who suspect foul play, interviewed three witnesses from the building: Larry, the building doorman; Anna, her next-door neighbor; and Timothy, the postman. When asked about the last interaction they had with Alexis, the witnesses gave the statements below:

**Larry:** "Alexis was a nice girl, normally very talkative, but she had been very quiet the past week or so before she vanished. I saw her come into the building at nearly 4 a.m. the morning of the 28th. She went straight to the elevator and up to the 5th floor where she lived without saying a word to me, which was unusual. She changed clothes and left the building just before 7 a.m. that same morning. No one has seen her since."

**Anna:** "Alexis is normally a great neighbor, but on the night of the 27th, she kept me awake all night with loud music coming from her apartment. I knocked on her door several times throughout the night but didn't get an answer. I thought I could hear her banging things around in her apartment through the wall. It was very annoying. The music didn't stop until just before my alarm went off to get up for work. I haven't seen or heard from her since."

**Timothy:** "I was delivering the mail around 6:50 a.m. on the 28th when I saw Alexis in the mail room. She looked very tired, and she mentioned she had only gotten home a few hours prior. She was expecting a package and asked me to check if I had anything for her. Sure enough there was a small box with her name on it. She put it in her bag and left the building right afterward."

After reviewing the witness statements, police were able to determine that one of the witnesses was lying, and subjected them to further investigation. Which witness was lying, and how did they know?

# THE PASSWORD PROBLEM

You're searching for evidence on the desktop computer of an associate at Reaver Realty Office as part of an ongoing murder investigation. But the computer is password protected, so you start searching for clues to uncover the password. Written in permanent ink on the bottom edge of the keyboard, you see an arrow pointing to the right with a number "1" next to it. Then, taped to the bottom of the keyboard, you find a sticky note with what looks like a cipher written on it. One of the words is **bolded**. Could this be the password?

RGW OWLALBRA ALT UR
UA RGW GIYBS ID RGW
**VLAJWECUKKWA** XLKKUBF DIE
URA OEWT. U'CW GWLES UR
IBXW IE RQUXW VWDIEW, VYR
BWCWE PYURW AI KIYS.

# LEAD DETECTIVE: ADVANCED PUZZLES

# SCENE OF THE CRIME

A crime scene has been tampered with. Detectives need your help finding what evidence has been removed or added since then. Compare the original photo with the current photo of the crime scene, and look out for 10 key differences.

# THE MILLIONAIRE MYSTERY

Millionaire Richard Handbrook disappeared early yesterday morning, and no one has seen him since. Was he kidnapped? Or worse? The only clue you have is some strange annotations left on a sticky note, stuck on a certain page in Handbrook's favorite book: *The Strange Case of Dr. Jekyll and Mr. Hyde.* Can you decipher the annotations and figure out if this is really a clue in the disappearance of Richard Handbrook?

1/2/5/3, 1/5/1/2, 1/8/7/6,

1/13/1/5, 1/20/6/1, 2/3/1/5,

2/5/3/7, 2/10/4/1, 2/14/1/1,

2/20/3/1, 3/5/6/2, 3/6/2/5,

3/12/2/1, 3/15/2/1, 3/18/6/2

"That's it!" said Poole. "It was this way. I came suddenly into the theatre from the garden. It seems he had slipped out to look for this drug or whatever it is; for the cabinet door was open, and there he was at the far end of the room digging among the crates. He looked up when I came in, gave a kind of cry, and whipped upstairs into the cabinet. It was but for one minute that I saw him, but the hair stood upon my head like quills. Sir, if that was my master, why had he a mask upon his face? If it was my master, why did he cry out like a rat, and run from me? I have served him long enough. And then..." The man paused and passed his hand over his face.

"These are all very strange circumstances," said Mr. Utterson, "but I think I begin to see daylight. Your master, Poole, is plainly seized with one of those maladies that both torture and deform the sufferer; hence, for aught I know, the

alteration of his voice; hence
the mask and the avoidance of his
friends; hence his eagerness to
find this drug, by means of which
the poor soul retains some hope
of ultimate recovery–God grant
that he be not deceived! There
is my explanation; it is sad
enough, Poole, ay, and appalling
to consider; but it is plain and
natural, hangs well together, and
delivers us from all exorbitant
alarms."

"Sir," said the butler, turning
to a sort of mottled pallor,
"that thing was not my master,
and there's the truth. My
master"–here he looked round him
and began to whisper–"is a tall,
fine build of a man, and this
was more of a dwarf." Utterson
attempted to protest. "O, sir,"
cried Poole, "do you think I do
not know my master after twenty
years? Do you think I do not know
where his head comes to in the
cabinet door, where I saw him
every morning of my life? No,
sir, that thing in the mask was
never Dr. Jekyll–God knows what

it was, but it was never Dr.
Jekyll; and it is the belief of
my heart that there was murder
done."

# MURDER AND MAYHEM

A series of murders have been committed, each at a different location across Brittany Beach, Delaware (an office, an amusement park, a residence, the boardwalk, and a warehouse), and each by a different suspect (Angel McFee, Damon Ryder, Moira Smiles, Ronda Wright, or Sirius Crumb). Detectives found blood evidence at each scene incriminating the suspects, who each have a different blood type (A+, AB+, B -, O+, and O-). Use the following clues to determine which suspect likely committed the murder at each location based on blood type, and which detective (Detective Apollo, Detective Castor, Detective Draco, Detective Leo, or Detective Rigel) conducted the investigation.

**1.** The suspects include Ronda Wright, the person suspected of the boardwalk murder, the person with A+ blood, and the person being investigated by Detective Rigel.

**2.** Detective Apollo discovered a sample of AB+ blood, but not at the residence, and it didn't match Moira Smiles.

**3.** Both Damon Ryder and Sirius Crumb have type O blood, and one of them is responsible for the murder in the warehouse.

**4.** The suspects include the person with B- blood, the person being investigated by Detective Draco, the person suspected of the office murder, and Angel McFee.

**5.** Detective Rigel did not find evidence implicating Sirius Crumb, Detective Apollo did not investigate the amusement park scene, and Detective Castor collected samples on the boardwalk.

**6.** Detective Draco found an O+ sample at the amusement park.

|  | LOCATION | | | | |
|---|---|---|---|---|---|
| | Office | Amusement Park | Residence | Boardwalk | Warehouse |
| **SUSPECT** Angel McFee | | | | | |
| Damon Ryder | | | | | |
| Moira Smiles | | | | | |
| Ronda Wright | | | | | |
| Sirius Crumb | | | | | |
| **INVESTIGATOR** Detective Apollo | | | | | |
| Detective Castor | | | | | |
| Detective Draco | | | | | |
| Detective Leo | | | | | |
| Detective Rigel | | | | | |
| **BLOOD TYPE** A+ | | | | | |
| AB+ | | | | | |
| B- | | | | | |
| O+ | | | | | |
| O- | | | | | |

| BLOOD TYPE | | | | | INVESTIGATOR | | | | |
|---|---|---|---|---|---|---|---|---|---|
| A+ | AB+ | B- | O+ | O- | Detective Apollo | Detective Castor | Detective Draco | Detective Leo | Detective Rigel |
| | | | | | | | | | |
| | | | | | | | | | |
| | | | | | | | | | |
| | | | | | | | | | |
| | | | | | | | | | |
| | | | | | | | | | |
| | | | | | | | | | |
| | | | | | | | | | |
| | | | | | | | | | |
| | | | | | | | | | |

# THE WELL-READ WHITLOCK KILLER

It's the spring of 1985, and a serial killer with a bizarre calling card is on the loose in Whitlock, Connecticut. The killer leaves cryptic notes containing vaguely threatening quotes from classic literature at each of his crime scenes. But when police rush to yet another crime scene on April 16th, they find that the note left by the killer this time doesn't make any sense. It seems to be gibberish, and no one has been able to solve it. A week later, at the latest serial killer crime scene, the killer leaves a new message, and it says "Today is key." With this new information, are you able to solve the mysterious code and find another clue that could lead you to catching this elusive serial killer?

DIODVI NSV, UMFDIT, WPNS M EDVSOX
YUQYE;

WQ PCHH XJH NFCX COT WEEEK WK
WSTGA XUVRDAXEH.

K ZIX NSV GMFD, CGW TNVMPJ EFS
RQW YZIXG:

WPNNO HRZ YHCUHTK, IJ ILNYEH YLBM
TLG SWBEV,

YKIY, LMHH ISD HGDBM DIPLMI MI, YDA
RY TNLOMT.

# COUNTING THE HOURS BEFORE DEATH

Change just one letter on each line to go from the top word to the bottom word. Do not change the order of the letters. You must have a common English word at each step.

HOURS

SOURS

SOARS

BOARS

BEARS

TEARS

PEARS

HEARS

HEATS

HEATH

DEATH

# UP IN FLAMES

A string of fires have broken out across town, and the police are trying to track down a possible arsonist. As the investigation progresses, the police headquarters suddenly start receiving strange coded messages in the mail. Could these messages be from the arsonist? Maybe they'll reveal a new clue in the case.

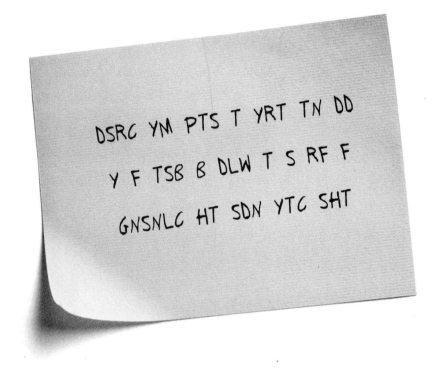

DSRC YM PTS T YRT TN DD

Y F TSB B DLW T S RF F

GNSNLC HT SDN YTC SHT

# BANKING ON AN ANSWER

There was an attempted robbery at Golden Bell Bank at 11 a.m. one morning. The suspect wore a mask to conceal their identity, and fled the scene soon after passing the bank teller a threatening message and demanding money. Police rounded up three possible suspects in the case: Robert, a former employee of Golden Bell Bank; Cameron, a local with a history of criminal activity; and David, the owner of a neighboring restaurant. When asked for their alibis during the time of the attempted robbery, they gave the witness statements below:

**Robert:** "I was supposed to pick up my final paycheck that morning, but I never made it in. I found a leak in my apartment and called a plumber immediately. I waited around at home trying to mitigate the damage before the plumber arrived just after 11:30 a.m."

**Cameron:** "I was driving around with my friends. We were in the area, but we didn't get into any trouble. My buddy stopped at the gas station across the street from the bank and filled up the car with fuel. That's the closest I was to the scene. After that, we drove across town to drop off our friend for work at the movie theater."

**David:** "I was at the restaurant in my office. I was on the phone, placing an order for more French wine, as that has been very popular with the restaurant lately. My customers have been requesting a great quantity of prosecco during dinner service, so that morning I placed a call to my distributor to order more. After that I was preparing for the upcoming lunch service at noon."

After reviewing the witness statements, police were able to determine that one of the suspects was lying about their alibi, and subjected them to further investigation. Which suspect was lying, and how did they know?

# THE CASE OF THE VINEYARD VACATION

You're investigating a murder at a local vineyard, where the victim was staying for a weeklong vacation. In the victim's room, you find a mysterious letter that seems to have some sort of code on it. Can you figure out what this secret message says?

Hello Dear,

In our last letter we discussed your poetry, and I agree with you. I'm also partial to odd sentences. They hold so much mystery and intrigue; I feel I could fill at least <u>15</u> books with <u>odd sentences</u> alone! The way they ebb and flow and describe the world through disjointed imagery. Simply beautiful. That's not to say there isn't something to be said for even sentences. Although a little more traditional and basic, they still bring about a simple beauty that one's writing is sure to need on occasion. Perhaps, I could only fill **9** books with such **even sentences**. But alas, it is true that a good mix of both is what is required to produce the very best work you

can. I'm so looking forward to
seeing what you and your trusty
pen come up with next!

Talk soon,
Your friend


Pgt ndj pagxvwi bn stpg?
Hxda ujbc vnbbjpn bxdwmnm bx
mrbcanbbnm, R'en knnw fxaarnm.
Iwt sxgtridg rdciprits bt, pcs
wt lpcih ndj id btti wxb pi
Hitaap Epgz dc Hpijgspn bdgcxcv.
R jv ngynlcrwp qrv cx xoona
vxan vxwnh, kdc R'v wxc bdan
fqjc pxxm rc fruu mx wxf. Jcstg
cd rxgrjbhipcrth pgt ndj id vd
padct. Vjtn bdan cqn kdcuna twxfb
jkxdc cqn yujw. Qt rpgtuja.

# A PAWS-ITIVELY PERFECT CRIME

Several expensive dogs were stolen from Chestnut Falls Veterinary Hospital during the night of June 7. The dogs that were stolen include a Samoyed, an English bulldog, and a Chow Chow. Police interviewed the following witnesses who were the last to have contact with the animals: Amber, a veterinary assistant; Dawn, a college student completing a summer internship at the hospital; and Toby, the owner of the English bulldog. They collected the following witness statements:

**Amber:** The three dogs that were taken were nearly fully recovered from their health issues. I know that the Chow Chow was in for hip dysplasia and the bulldog was recovering from surgery. Copies of their breed certification paperwork were stolen as well, so whoever did this intends to sell them for high prices. I last saw the dogs the afternoon of June 7 when I was working in the office. The veterinarian mentioned to me that all three dogs would likely be released from our care the following day.

**Dawn:** I loved working with those sweet dogs! The Chow Chow with the bad hip was my favorite—she would always stick out her big pink tongue when I brought food to the kennels. I gave all the animals food and water the evening of June 7, before I left the office for the night. When I returned the next morning to open the front door for the day, their kennel doors were open and the dogs were missing.

**Toby:** This is a very expensive animal hospital and I never expected something like this to happen. Reginald, my English bulldog, has been with me for nearly six years. When I took him in for surgery last week they said everything went well and he was recovering nicely. He was set to come home on June 8th.

After reviewing the witness statements, police were able to determine that one of the witnesses was lying, and subjected them to further questioning. Which witness was lying, and how did they know?

# THE COMMENT CONUNDRUM

A string of murders by strangulation have the police searching everywhere for the serial killer, now called the Salt Wells Strangler. Suddenly, a person claiming to be the Strangler leaves a comment under a seemingly random online news article for a well-known science publication. You're hoping this message could help you catch the Strangler once and for all, but it looks like part of the message is in some kind of code. Using the clues you've gathered so far, can you find the answer?

### A Reimagined Order to the Alphabet

## N X A C M E Y R H D L W Z Q T K J I G S U B O V P F

Scientists have recently discovered a group of people who have learned the alphabet in a particular order that is much different than the typical "ABC" order widely accepted and used in the English language. The people were found to....

**Anonymous** a minute ago

It's me, the one and only Strangler. It's a pity how *backwards* everything has gotten, but I'll give you a clue. Catch me if you can!

Vw wiu ocgfug cn fcgwi vfj yuocfj, v bhjjvs yivjct guvoiuy hwy xuvl. Nckkct wiu fvbu vw wiu yebbhw, vfj sce thkk nhfj tivw sce yuul.

  REPLY

# STOLEN GOODS STORAGE

A group of thieves has been purchasing sheds and placing them at different locations in order to hide stolen goods before selling them on the black market. Thus far, undercover detectives have determined that the thieves have a total of five sheds, each with a different length (10, 11, 12, 13, or 14 feet) and width (5, 6, 7, 8, or 9 feet), and each placed at a different location (ranch house, abandoned farm, in the woods, vacant lot, or under the freeway). Detectives suspect that each of the five different stolen items (jewelry, fine china, antique chair, computer, bicycle) will be located in one of the sheds, and each item has a different estimated value ($1,100, $1,200, $1,300, $1,400, or $1,500). Use the clues to determine the location and dimensions of each shed, as well as what stolen item it houses and the value of that item. (Note: Area in square feet is the product of length times width.)

**1.** The $1,200 jewelry (which isn't stashed in the shed in the woods) is in a shed with an area of exactly 65 square feet. The shed housing the antique chair isn't 12 feet long.

**2.** The shed on the vacant lot (which is exactly 90 square feet) houses a stolen item worth $200 less than the antique chair.

**3.** The stolen item worth $1,400 (which isn't the bicycle) is stored in a shed with exactly 88 square feet of space.

**4.** The stolen computer (which is stored in the abandoned farm shed) is worth neither $1,100 nor $1,400.

**5.** The antique chair is stored in the ranch house shed, which has the same square footage of at least one other shed.

| | | LENGTH | | | | | WIDTH | | | | |
|---|---|---|---|---|---|---|---|---|---|---|---|
| | | 10 feet | 11 feet | 12 feet | 13 feet | 14 feet | 5 feet | 6 feet | 7 feet | 8 feet | 9 feet |
| **STOLEN ITEM** | Jewelry | | | | | | | | | | |
| | Fine china | | | | | | | | | | |
| | Antique chair | | | | | | | | | | |
| | Computer | | | | | | | | | | |
| | Bicycle | | | | | | | | | | |
| **VALUE OF ITEM** | $1,100 | | | | | | | | | | |
| | $1,200 | | | | | | | | | | |
| | $1,300 | | | | | | | | | | |
| | $1,400 | | | | | | | | | | |
| | $1,500 | | | | | | | | | | |
| **LOCATION** | Ranch house | | | | | | | | | | |
| | Abandoned farm | | | | | | | | | | |
| | In the woods | | | | | | | | | | |
| | Vacant lot | | | | | | | | | | |
| | Under the freeway | | | | | | | | | | |
| **WIDTH** | 5 feet | | | | | | | | | | |
| | 6 feet | | | | | | | | | | |
| | 7 feet | | | | | | | | | | |
| | 8 feet | | | | | | | | | | |
| | 9 feet | | | | | | | | | | |

| | | LOCATION | | | | | VALUE OF ITEM | | |
|---|---|---|---|---|---|---|---|---|---|
| Ranch house | Abandoned farm | In the woods | Vacant lot | Under the freeway | $1,100 | $1,200 | $1,300 | $1,400 | $1,500 |
| | | | | | | | | | |
| | | | | | | | | | |
| | | | | | | | | | |
| | | | | | | | | | |
| | | | | | | | | | |
| | | | | | | | | | |
| | | | | | | | | | |
| | | | | | | | | | |
| | | | | | | | | | |
| | | | | | | | | | |

# A KILLER STRIKES AGAIN

The following cryptogram puzzle was published in the want ads of the *Copper Cliffs Community Catalogue*. Local area law enforcement determined it was a message from the serial killer Matty Marks. Can you decode the message?

---

V YVPP AVPP BWBVT ZTPHMM XSZ JBNJE
QH RVIMN. VR XSZ RBVP XSZ YVPP RVTC
B FSCX ST NEH RISTN MNHKM SR NEH
JSKKHI JPVRRM JSZINESZMH FZN STPX
BRNHI V'UH MAVKKHC NSYT.

---

# THE HOTEL HOMICIDE

A body was found in room 512 at the Bluegill Hotel. Police have determined the man's cause of death to be a homicide. Investigators questioned three individuals who were on the hotel premises the night of the murder: Hillary, a hotel housekeeper who discovered the victim; Jacob, a guest staying in a neighboring room; and Rebecca, the victim's sister and the last person who had contact with him. They collected the following witness statements:

**Hillary:** I knocked on the door of room 512 in the afternoon to do the housekeeping. No one answered, so I entered the room. I turned off the TV, switched on the lights, and began to straighten up the bedroom. One of the light bulbs had burned out in the lamp, so I replaced it. I also restocked the minibar, which was missing several small bottles of liquor. When I got to the bathroom, I found the man's body.

**Jacob:** I didn't hear any loud noises or sounds of a struggle from across the hall that night. At one point I did hear the door open and someone go into the room. When I went later that night to get ice from the vending room at around 7:30 p.m., I noticed the door was slightly ajar and there was light and the sound of a TV coming into the hallway. Sounded like they were watching the Lakers game on TV. When I left my room the next morning, the door was fully closed, so I didn't think anything of it.

**Rebecca:** After getting a call to come to the hotel, I went to see my brother. He was in room 512, which I thought was funny because that was our old area code when we lived in Los Angeles growing up. It was so good to see him, even though he said he would be leaving town the next morning. We had a few drinks from the minibar and watched TV together, just like old times. I left at around 10 p.m. It was the last time I saw him.

After reviewing the witness statements, police were able to determine that one of the witnesses was lying, and subjected them to further investigation. Which witness was lying, and how did the police know?

# SOLUTIONS

# ASPIRING SLEUTH: BEGINNER PUZZLES

## THE FLIP PHONE CONUNDRUM, page 24
**Solution:** WIRE THE MONEY FIRST OF DECEMBER. USE THIS PHONE TO CONTACT XAVIER.

**Key:** Use the phone keypad to decipher the code. The first number in each hyphenated pair refers to the number on the phone, and the second number corresponds to which letter on the number pad it is. For example, 9-1 is the letter *W*.

## TRIPLE HOMICIDE AT THE SUNSET MOTEL, page 26
Tracy Gray is the female victim, and she's wearing a brown shirt. Skyler Green is wearing a gray shirt, and Alex Brown is wearing a green shirt.

## "CRIME TIME," page 28

| CRIMINAL | JUDGE | SENTENCE |
|----------|-------|----------|
| Clyde Danger | Judge Campbell | 7 years |
| Micky Mongoose | Judge Garcia | 5 years |
| Florida Rose | Judge Brown | 1 year |
| Teddy Oswald | Judge Anderson | 3 years |
| Patty Manson | Judge Lee | 10 years |

## GUNNING FOR ANSWERS, page 30
**Solution:** RAIN FALLS IN THE EAST WHEN THE BIRDS STOP CHIRPING

**Key:** The alphabet is reversed. So A=Z, B=Y, C=X, and so on.

## SHOT TO DEATH, page 34

Mrs. Fontaine is lying. She claims to have heard the shot at 9:15 p.m., but it took 15 minutes for Dr. Fontaine to drive home, and he left work at 9:08.

## A PLAN TO KILL, page 37

Answers may vary. PLAN, flan, flat, feat, felt, fell, fill, KILL

## CRIME AT COPPER CLIFFS, page 38

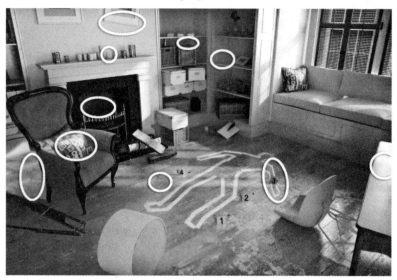

## THE ART OF THE CRIME, page 40

**Solution:** "MY UNCLE IS FRAMING ME. CHECK HIS SAFETY DEPOSIT BOX AT GOLDEN BELL BANK. YOU WILL FIND SOME OF THE MISSING ART STOLEN FROM MY MOTHER WHEN SHE DIED."

**Key:** Caesar shift—Each letter of the alphabet is shifted 7 places

## MURDER GONE A-RYE, page 42
**Solution:** James Smith on Willow Street

**Key:** Use the date as the shift key—put the six numbers in the date over each letter of the coded message, repeating the numbers until all letters have a number.

| 0 | 2 | 0 | 8 | 7 | 3 | 0 | 2 | 0 | 8 | 7 | 3 | 0 | 2 | 0 | 8 | 7 | 3 | 0 | 2 | 0 | 8 | 7 | 3 |
|---|---|---|---|---|---|---|---|---|---|---|---|---|---|---|---|---|---|---|---|---|---|---|---|
| J | C | M | M | Z | V | M | K | T | P | V | Q | W | K | L | T | V | Z | S | V | R | M | L | W |

Each number indicates how many times a certain letter has been shifted from its original place in the alphabet. So to decode it, you have to shift the letter backward that many spaces. For example, the first letter in the cipher, *J*, has been assigned a 0, meaning it was not shifted. The next letter, *C*, was assigned a 2, meaning it had been shifted two spaces in the alphabet from its original letter. Therefore, this letter is supposed to be *A*.

## WRITTEN IN BLOOD, page 44

| Solution: | Complete Key: | |
|---|---|---|
| SEE NO EVIL | A = & | R = % |
| HEAR NO EVIL | E = ^ | V = / |
| SPEAK NO EVIL | K = # | S = > |
| | L = ! | O = < |
| | N = + | I = $ |
| | P = ~ | H = ? |

## SOMEONE IS GUILTY—BAR NONE, page 46

Alexa is lying. She claims she did not drink any hard liquor that night, though the other suspects claim she ordered a Long Island Iced Tea, which contains rum, vodka, tequila, gin, and triple sec.

## THE MOTEL MYSTERY, page 48

**Solution:** The shipment should be ready at four in the morning on Saturday. Let the boss know.

**Key:** All vowels are removed.

## CYBER WARFARE, page 50

**Solution:** I am what men fear. I am the Giant Killer.

**Key:** The dates tell you how to decode the passage and find the secret message. The first number in the date represents a line of text, the second number represents the word in that line.

## SUSPICIOUS SALES, page 52

Danielle is lying. She claims the suspect left in a minivan. Her son Johnny did not count any minivans in the parking lot at that time. Both Alex and Johnny hear the suspect leave and make a lot of noise in the parking lot, implying he left on the motorcycle.

# PRIVATE INVESTIGATOR: INTERMEDIATE PUZZLES

ESCAPE THE MAZE, page 56

## ART OF THE STEAL, page 58

**Solution:** Grove storage unit nine

**Key:** First number represents a line in the poem, second number represents the word in that line, third number represents the letter in that word.

## A MURDERER, WITH BLOOD ON THEIR HANDS, FRETS, page 60

Answers may vary. BLOOD, brood, broad, bread, tread, treed, trees, frees, FRETS

## TERROR POSTSCRIPT, page 61
**Solution:**

October fifteenth will be big

But before then

Catch me if you can.

**Key:** Since this mystery is taking place in England, the date September 25, 2016, would appear in writing as 25/09/16, with the day coming before the month. This is the key to the cipher. Use the date as the shift key—put the six numbers in the date over each letter of the coded message, repeating the number until all letters have a number. These numbers indicate how many times that letter has been shifted from its original place in the alphabet. So to decode it, you have to shift the letter backward that many spaces.

## THE BAFFLING BANK CODE, page 62

**Solution:** June eleventh seems a fine day for some fun in the area. The security system is being repaired at noon and the cameras will be down. But only for ten minutes, then back to normal. A lock on the back door has also been giving maintenance some problems lately.

**Key:** All vowels are removed.

## LATE NIGHT AT THE LIBRARY, page 66

Alana is lying. She mentions three Jane Austen novels, but *The Tenant of Wildfell Hall* was written by Anne Brontë, not Jane Austen.

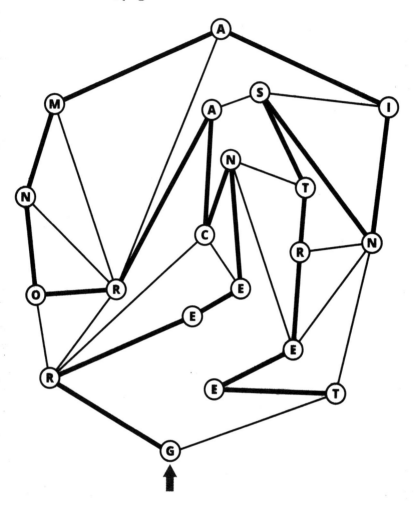

## TRICK OR TREAT, page 70

**Solution:** Why, oh why, must you celebrate Halloween? The worst holiday of the year is meant to be observed in silence and without fanfare. The festival must stop. Or else.

**Key:** The alphabet is reversed. So A=Z, B=Y, C=X, and so on.

## NOT JAKE MORGAN!!!, page 71

**Solution:** PLACE ONE MILLION DOLLARS IN SMALL UNMARKED BILLS NEXT TO PERRY'S MONUMENT IN LAKE ERIE, PENNSYLVANIA, BY MIDNIGHT TONIGHT, OR YOUR BOY JAKE IS DEAD.

**Key:** (coded letter = original letter)

| | | |
|---|---|---|
| A = X | J = H | S = A |
| B = F | K = J | T = E |
| C = O | L = Z | U = S |
| D = U | M = B | V = G |
| E = P | N = M | W = L |
| F = Q | O = N | X = K |
| G = I | P = V | Y = C |
| H = W | Q = R | Z = T |
| I = D | R = Y | |

## AFTERNOON ALIBIS, page 72

| CRIMINAL | CRIME | ALIBI | TIME OF CRIME |
|----------|-------|-------|---------------|
| Frederick | Assault | Work | 2:00 p.m. |
| Mary | Forgery | Party | 4:00 p.m. |
| Eliza | Arson | None | 3:00 p.m. |
| Jonathan | Theft | Date | 5:00 p.m. |
| Mark | Murder | Parents | 1:00 p.m. |

## CURVEBALL CRIME, page 76

**Solution:** One hundred thousand for help with Ricks

**Key:** Use the chart showing all the positions, and fill it in with a keypad-like layout based on where the ABC starts in the chart drawing attached to the email. Also follow the batting order directions in the email that say, "Once a first batter is designated, we simply follow the order of positions as listed above, going left to right, top to bottom." Map out the keypad based on those clues.

| | | |
|---|---|---|
| P—JKL | C—MNO | FB—PQR |
| SB—STU | TB—VWX | SS—YZ |
| LF—ABC | CF—DEF | RF—GHI |

## GONE IN A NEW YORK MINUTE, page 79

Anna lied in her witness statement. Both Larry and Timothy corroborated that Alexis did not get home until very early on the morning of the 28th. Since she lived alone, it is not possible that she or anyone else was home to make noise on the night of the 27th.

## THE PASSWORD PROBLEM, page 81

**Solution:** THE PEASANTS SAY IT IS THE HOUND OF THE **BASKERVILLES** CALLING FOR ITS PREY. I'VE HEARD IT ONCE OR TWICE BEFORE, BUT NEVER QUITE SO LOUD.

Password is **BASKERVILLES**.

**Key:** Keyboard Shift—Arrow pointing to the right with the number *1* indicates you should shift every letter of the keyboard 1 space to the right on a standard QWERTY computer keyboard. At the end of a row, when shifting 1 space to the right, you will land at the beginning of the same row.

# LEAD DETECTIVE: ADVANCED PUZZLES

## SCENE OF THE CRIME, page 84

## THE MILLIONAIRE MYSTERY, page 86
**Solution:** Don't try to find me

**Key:** First number represents the paragraph, second represents the line, third represents the word, fourth represents the letter.

## MURDER AND MAYHEM, page 90

| SUSPECT | LOCATION | BLOOD TYPE | INVESTIGATOR |
|---------|----------|------------|--------------|
| Angel McFee | Residence | A+ | Detective Leo |
| Damon Ryder | Warehouse | O- | Detective Rigel |
| Moira Smiles | Boardwalk | B- | Detective Castor |
| Ronda Wright | Office | AB+ | Detective Apollo |
| Sirius Crumb | Amusement Park | O+ | Detective Draco |

## THE WELL-READ WHITLOCK KILLER, page 94
### Solution:

Demand not, Reader; this I cannot write;

So much the fact all reach of words surpassed.

I was not dead, yet living was not quite:

Think for thyself, if gifted with the power,

What, life and death denied me, was my plight.

(from *The Divine Comedy* of Dante Alighieri, public domain)

**Key:** You know the year is 1985, and that it's April. You're given one date: April 16th. But the message that says "Today is key" appears a week after this date. Thus, that message appears on April 23, 1985. Therefore, "Today is key" refers to the date 04/23/85, and it means that this date is the key used to solve the previous coded message. Thus, you can infer that the coded message is a date cipher.

To solve, put the six numbers in the date 04/23/85 over each letter of the coded message, repeating the number until all letters have a number. These numbers indicate how many times that letter has been shifted from its original place in the alphabet. So to decode it, you have to shift the letter backward that many spaces.

## COUNTING THE HOURS BEFORE DEATH, page 96

Answers may vary. HOURS, sours, soars, boars, board, beard, bears, beats, heats, heath, DEATH

## UP IN FLAMES, page 97

**Solution:** This city needs the cleansing of fire so it would be best if you did not try to stop my crusade.

**Key:** Text is written backward, then all the vowels are removed.

## BANKING ON AN ANSWER, page 98

David is lying about his alibi. Prosecco is not a French wine, so his phone order story does not add up.

## THE CASE OF THE VINEYARD VACATION, page 100

**Solution:** Are you alright my dear? Your last message sounded so distressed, I've been worried. The director contacted me, and he wants you to meet him at Stella Park on Saturday morning. I am expecting him to offer more money, but I'm not sure what good it will do now. Under no circumstances are you to go alone. Make sure the butler knows about the plan. Be careful.

**Key:** The underlined words "odd sentences" and the underlined number "15" determine that all odd number sentences of the cipher are made by shifting each letter of the alphabet 15 places. The bold "even sentences" and number "9" indicate that all even numbered sentences are made by shifting each letter of the alphabet 9 places. So every other sentence of the cipher is decoded with a different shift cipher.

## A PAWS-ITIVELY PERFECT CRIME, page 102

Dawn is lying. She mentioned her favorite animal was the Chow Chow with the pink tongue, but the Chow Chow breed is known for their blue-black colored tongues.

## THE COMMENT CONUNDRUM, page 104

**Solution:** At the corner of north and second, a midday shadow reaches its peak. Follow the name at the summit, and you will find what you seek.

**Key:** Instead of using the normal alphabet order of "ABC," use the order of the alphabet as seen in the scientific article to help decode the message. Then, in the Strangler's comment, the word "backwards" is italicized. Therefore, you can deduce that the code uses the new alphabet order, and that the Strangler is using that alphabet backward. So for the code, N=F, X=P, A=V, and so on.

Here's the new alphabet in bold, with the reverse above it:

| F | P | V | O | B | U | S | G | I | J | K | T | Q |
|---|---|---|---|---|---|---|---|---|---|---|---|---|
| **N** | **X** | **A** | **C** | **M** | **E** | **Y** | **R** | **H** | **D** | **L** | **W** | **Z** |

| Z | W | L | D | H | R | Y | E | M | C | A | X | N |
|---|---|---|---|---|---|---|---|---|---|---|---|---|
| **Q** | **T** | **K** | **J** | **I** | **G** | **S** | **U** | **B** | **O** | **V** | **P** | **F** |

## STOLEN GOODS STORAGE, page 106

| STOLEN ITEM | LENGTH | WIDTH | LOCATION | VALUE OF ITEM |
|---|---|---|---|---|
| Jewelry | 13 feet | 5 feet | Under the freeway | $1,200 |
| Fine china | 11 feet | 8 feet | In the woods | $1,400 |
| Antique chair | 14 feet | 6 feet | Ranch house | $1,300 |
| Computer | 12 feet | 7 feet | Abandoned farm | $1,500 |
| Bicycle | 10 feet | 9 feet | Vacant lot | $1,100 |

## A KILLER STRIKES AGAIN, page 110

**Solution:** I WILL KILL AGAIN UNLESS YOU CATCH ME FIRST. IF YOU FAIL YOU WILL FIND A BODY ON THE FRONT STEPS OF THE COPPER CLIFFS COURTHOUSE BUT ONLY AFTER I'VE SKIPPED TOWN.

Key: This is a substitution puzzle where each letter stands for another letter (and the substitution is completely random). To start, notice that the only one-letter words are V and B. They must correspond to I and A. Since later there is a "V'UH," V is most likely I, and B is then A. You can then deduce that U, H must be V, E, so that "V'UH" = "I'VE."

From there, identifying other two-letter and three-letter words becomes easier. (It's a safe guess that "NEH" is "THE," that "VR" must be "if," "in," or "is.") It takes a bit of puzzling to figure out the rest, but given time you can suss out the remaining letters (coded letter = original letter).

| | | |
|---|---|---|
| A = K | J = C | S = O |
| B = A | K = P | T = N |
| C = D | L = X | U = V |
| D = J | M = S | V = I |
| E = H | N = T | W = G |
| F = B | O = Z | X = Y |
| G = Q | P = L | Y = W |
| H = E | Q = M | Z = U |
| I = R | R = F | |

## THE HOTEL HOMICIDE, page 111

Rebecca was lying. 512 is the area code for Austin, Texas, and not Los Angeles, California.

# ABOUT

Since 2016, Hunt A Killer has disrupted conventional forms of storytelling by delivering physical items, documents, and puzzles to tell immersive stories that bring friends and families together. What started as an in-person event has now grown into a thriving entertainment company with over 100,000 subscribers and over four million boxes shipped. Hunt A Killer creates shared experiences and community for those seeking unique ways to socialize and challenge themselves.